DON'T BE "THAT" PATIENT
By
Ann Williams

For
Esther Chin, who always believes in me

And For

Travis Key, who kept me laughing when we worked in Hell

Preface

Not to offend anyone, but first and foremost, Fuck is my first language. This book will be full of Fucks, mostly Fucks not given. So, if you are not good with Fuck, or any sort of fucking, then you should not read any further....

You will also read a lot of "Don'ts" or "Do nots." If you are not up for that either, no need to go any further.

You can look at this book as a handbook of how to survive your next doctor's visit because in short, we are done with your shit. Of course, I am speaking for myself when I say, "we," but I really mean the hundreds and thousands of physician's offices across the country that put up with all the rude and ungrateful patients daily.

I have a been a patient from time to time, as I am sure everyone has, but I have never acted or behaved the way patients, i.e., you, the public act towards a staff member or any medical professional of a medical practice.

Now, I know what you are thinking. You are thinking this is just some front desk, snotty little receptionist ranting. It is not. I am going to lay it all out for you, so you can fully understand where I am coming from.

You all have come from the Land of Entitlement and think we, "The Office" owe you something. Let me be the first one to tell you, we owe you nothing.

Nothing. Nada, zilch, zippo.

I have worked for many doctors; primary care doctors, pediatricians, infertility doctors, dermatologists, ER doctors, pulmonologists, psychiatrists (and yes, their patients are nuts, but not as crazy as the doctors!) and all kinds of other specialists, truly, I have run the gamut. I have started at the bottom and been to the top. This little handbook of sorts will help you navigate your next doctors' office visit with great ease and will have the staff loving you, if you behave accordingly, that is.

We are terribly busy. We care for you, our beloved patients. And here is how it starts ~

The Phone Call

Our phones are ringing off the hook and I am sorry we must ask you to hold. Yes, we have seven incoming lines and five people to answer them, however, this is not the only thing the front desk is doing, or anyone else in the office for that matter. They are not waiting for you to call them. Therefore, we ask you to hold. We ask you to hold because we are checking in our other beloved patients, you know the ones that come in and scream at us in person and give us attitude in person whereas you are just giving us shit over the phone about being put on hold.

Now, you want an appointment, but you do not know when you want to come in. So

 what the fuck did you call for? Please get your shit together before you call. We would all be so grateful if you would do this. When you want to make an appointment, shouldn't you know the day and time you want to come in?

Honestly, we offer you every God Damn time, day, hour, we have, and you just tell us, "No that's not good, Suzie has piano," "Bobby has soccer," "I have to take my dog to the vet." Guess what, we do not give a fuck. We just want to make a God Damn appointment for you and get you off the line, so we can move on to the next beloved patient.

 Now I can see you thinking to yourself, "Well, they never have the time and day I want, when I call." My response is this rarely happens. We as medical professionals always try to accommodate our patients unless you are an asshole to us.

I want you to really think about this when you call us, because if you call us and have attitude and are a total fucking asshole, and this goes for you ladies as well; if I answer the phone and I have an appointment, you know the one you are asking for and you're still being an asshole to me, that will be the last one on the planet I offer you.

In short, be nice.

Really, I wish this is where the call ended, but sadly, it does not end here because we then must ask for some pertinent information, which would be, easy things you should know. Like your name. Ok this is an easy one. You just give us your name, not ten versions of it, just your fucking name. We do not need to know, you just got divorced from your bastardly husband that had six women on the side, and now has three kids with each of them, we just want your name. We just need your first name and last name. That is it.

Do not tell us that you, just got married and one ID has your married name on it and the other ID has your single name on it, because for us, that is a problem. One, if you do not know who the fuck you are, how are we going to know.... Just saying. It is also a problem for us, because if your ID and your insurance card do not match up, most offices are going to tell you to hit the road, but in nicer terms.

 This is because we need to verify your identity, and as you have read in the lines above, you already do not know who the fuck you are and neither do we.

 Next, we must ask you for your address, phone number, and date of birth. Again, this is all information YOU know! We need you to remember who you are, where you live and how old you are when you call the office to make an appointment, let alone when you want your appointment! This information is not needed by just our office, every physician's office you call is going to ask you for this shit.

Your insurance information is next, we ask you this, because, if we do not take your insurance, then you will have to pay for the visit, and no one wants that! I think you, the patient, should know what kind of insurance you carry and if you do not, you are an idiot. Knowing what kind of insurance, you carry is an integral part of making the appointment. Do not call us and make us try and figure out what kind of policy you fucking signed up for when we have no idea, six lines are ringing, we are checking patients in and out and you are staring at the fucking card that says "HMO" on it, but you tell us it's a "PPO". In short this makes us insane.

Do you know enough about your insurance plan to know that you need a referral to see a specialist, because that is what we are and if you do not have a referral from your PCP – short for primary care physician, then you have not only screwed yourself, but you have also screwed us! More on this later.

Before ending the call, we ask you to confirm your phone number. Do not lie to us and give us a bogus number. This hurts you more than us. Honestly, we could give two fucks less if our automated calling center/text system reminds you of your appointment or not, but if you do not give us the right phone number then you are never going to get the reminder call/text about your appointment that we've just spent fifteen fucking minutes making with you and when you miss it, that will just give you one more reason to bitch at us.

Holy Christ, I am exhausted just from that one chapter, can you imagine what it is like taking the fucking phone call?!

Rescheduling

I know you are not going to believe this, but we hate calling you almost as much as you hate hearing from us to reschedule an appointment. But let us be honest here, you as patients call us all the time and reschedule your appointments so turnabout is fair play. My point on this, is do not get all snappy on us when we call you to reschedule your appointment. You call us because your life gets in the way of your appointment or your son's appointment or whatever. Well, believe it or not, doctors, nurse practitioners, physician assistants, they all have these things called "lives."

Reminder Calls and Text Reminders

Reminder calls and text messaging are made as a courtesy. When you are called, please do not act like it is a major interruption of your fucking day. We do this to not only remind you of your appointment but to ensure that our schedules are full.

Text messaging, this is a bit of sore spot for me. When you get a text message from us, it asks you to confirm the appointment. Just be a responsible person and hit "yes" or "confirm." Do not be a fucktard and just look at the text message reminder and be like, "oh I have an appointment on Monday." If you do not confirm the appointment, then we must call you to make sure you know that you have an appointment. Confirm the God Damn appointment!!

Forms

These will keep you busy while you are in the waiting room. The form to update your information is three pages long. We have printed it out in larger print; therefore, it is three pages long. I would like to tell you, I am sorry you must fill it out, but I am not. You see, I also must fill out forms and all sorts of paperwork when I go to my doctor, so quit bitching about it and just fill the fucking thing out.

"Same" Do not put this on the form. You know why? Because, if we do not have your right information, then it is not the fucking "same"!!! The form will be returned to you, to fill it out correctly. "Same" also does not work if you have thirty-seven children. If we are seeing eight of your children, then eight forms must be filled out. This is not our problem; this is your problem. Quit having sex. This is where saying, "No," comes into play. All eight forms are required to be filled out. Do not come to us, at the front desk and tell us you are not prepared to fill out the form, it is not a fucking test.

Do not ask us after you have filled out one page if you must fill out the other two pages. Yes, you must fill out the entire fucking form. Everyone fills out the form. Everyone. If you could not finish it in the waiting room, and you could not finish it in the exam room, then we will give you an envelope, you can take it home and fill It out at your leisure and mail it back. If you do not mail it back and you come in again, you will again be asked to fill it out. It is truly a vicious cycle, and we are good at winning at it.

Signing the form

Everyone signs the form. If you do not want to sign the form, then you are brought into my office and really you do not want this, because when you are brought into my office, I am not going to put up with your shit, because in short, I do not give a fuck why you do not want to sign the form.

You either sign it and be seen or you leave. It is really that easy. Do not alter the form. Do not for one second, even think you are going to cross out our words and put in your own bull shit then sign it. You will be given a new form.

Also, do not try to tell me, that we are the only doctor's office that makes your fill out forms. This is fucking bullshit. I will tell you the same thing when you are standing in front of me.

If you are a total asshole to me, I will bring you on a little field trip next door to the dentist and ask them if they make their patients fill out forms, so you know, it is not just us. Quit wasting our time and fill out the fucking form.

The Waiting Room

This is where you are going to wait for your appointment. We have nice furniture, magazines, which we keep updated for your reading pleasure. We keep it nice; we keep it clean.

If you are not happy with the magazine selection we offer, please do not go to the front desk, and ask them if we have anything else to read. You are not at the fucking library or a bookstore, you are at the Doctor's office and as much as we want you to be entertained while you wait for your provider, if you are not happy with our reading selection, then you should bring your own selection of reading material. If you ask to see the office manager, i.e., me, I will tell you the same thing. Also, do not tell me that you do not like our magazines. I do not give fuck. There are literally five thousand different magazines out there, find one, sit the fuck down and shut the fuck up and wait for your appointment like a respectable person.

Cleanliness. We expect you to respect that we have kept the "waiting room" clean for you, our beloved patients. We hate gross, used Kleenex on the floor, that you, our beloved patients, for some reason cannot seem to pick up after you have dropped it on the floor. Please pick it up along with any other trash you have felt the need to just discard on the floor. I cannot understand why you would just leave it on the floor. Do you do this at your house? That is so disgusting. Unfortunately for me, it is my job to pick it up off the floor and after that lovely snot has dried to the floor, it makes it a little difficult to get if off the floors. Do not worry, I have on rubber gloves, because, I have been down this disgusting road before, with your children's gum. You know the gum, that they have strategically placed on the back of our nice dark cherry wood chairs and that our so -called cleaning company has missed along with those fucking sucked on suckers we hand out at the end of every visit (another very sore spot with me). I would really appreciate it if you as parents would watch your children. What a concept, but then I think they are just an extension of you and have just watched you drop that gross Kleenex to the floor and with your foot, bat it under the chair. A no win situation for me. I would like to take this opportunity to tell you, we have these things called "trash cans", just ask, we can show you where they are. We can even show you and your family how to use them.

The Stereo or the television. These have been placed in the waiting room for all the patients to enjoy not just for your enjoyment. Please do not touch them or change the channels on them. Please do not come to the front desk and ask for the remote, please do not ask us to change the station on the stereo. Just suck it up and sit in your fucking seat and wait for your appointment.

"Waiting" in the waiting room. Please do not come in my office and bitch at me because you had to "wait" for your appointment. You are kidding right? Do not be an absolute fucking bitch to me and tell me you had to wait for forty minutes because we were running late. After hearing this, I almost do not know how to respond. Yet, I am the office manager and I have all the answers...I tell you that sometimes procedures run longer and that we do our best to see everyone and give every patient the necessary time and care needed at the time of service. That is how it is. We try to treat you with respect and take care of your problems. Now if you are gonna be a nasty bitch to me and tell me that our scheduling girls do not know how to schedule then threaten me that you are not going to come back because you must wait, well then see you later bitch and we will make sure you must wait every single fucking time you show up. Oh, and your doctor that you see, has been informed of all this too.

Wi-Fi Password

Yes, we have one and yes, we will give it to you. Please do not ask the front desk if you can use the same wi-fi that the office uses, because the answer will always be NO. We offer free wi-fi to our patients but if you are coming into the office to do your personal banking on-line, or some online human or drug trafficking business, while you are waiting for your appointment, I would rethink this plan.

Day Care

We are not running one. So, do not even think for one fucking millisecond, you are going to leave your children out in the "waiting room" unsupervised. Do not even ask us to watch your child, the answer is NO, will always be NO and will NEVER be yes. Toys, we do not have any. You know why? Because we are not a fucking daycare.

Back in the day, when I worked for the pediatricians, moms & dads just left their kids unattended in the waiting room and told their kids to be good and acted like we had nothing better to do than watch their God Damn kid while the other one was screaming in the exam room. I will tell you the minute parents left their child alone in the waiting room it became Satan.

The Appointment

The magical day has arrived. Be on time. What does this mean? Most doctors' offices these days will tell you, that you must be on time, if you are fifteen minutes or more, late, your appointment will need to be rescheduled. We fall into the do not be late or we will have to reschedule "your" category.

 I know, I can already hear you saying to yourself, (with a little attitude, no doubt) "Why do I need to show up early when I'm just going to end up sitting in the waiting room thirty minutes past my appointment." My reply is this is a doctor's office. Yes, we really do try to run on time, but shit happens. And you know what else happens? Emergencies. Emergencies happen.

 If someone is bleeding and you are just in for a blood pressure check, you are going to sit there regardless of who arrived first. So please do not come up to the front desk to tell us you were there before the kid that was bleeding profusely from his cracked head, left a trail of blood in the waiting room and was screaming in pain, because you will sit there for what seems like eternity. In fact, you may just sit out there until you are fucking dead.

Doctors, nurses, medical assistants, physician assistants and nurse practitioners, as well as administrative staff are all doing their best to take care of you, but it all takes time, and let me remind all of you from the Land of Entitlement, which think your problems outweigh everyone else's on the planet. Quit thinking of yourself for a change.

When the medical assistant calls you out of the waiting room, be nice. We realize that you have had to wait, but we have now brought you back into the chaos that you could not see in the waiting room, and this should be your first clue of what is really going on in this place. It always makes me laugh, when I hear in passing from a patient, "Wow, it's really busy back here." No shit. Hence the reason you have been in the waiting room for half an hour. Jesus Christ. And still clueless.

You are now placed in a room with a medical assistant, who is going to check your vital signs, if it is that type of physician, or they are going to weigh you, etc. You pretty much know the routine, here. We have questions to ask you, that only you have the answers to. Please do not lie to us. We will find out eventually and it will not make us happy. When we ask you to confirm your date of birth, we are not doing this for our health, our medical staff are pulling your information out of our electronic data base and we want to make sure it is really you, so lose the fucking attitude and just tell the medical assistant your fucking date of birth and do it with a God Damn smile. Now that we know who you are, we can continue with the visit.

Let us pretend, I am a medical assistant, who I am not, but just so you know, I have been one and as a medical assistant, as part of my job, I must ask you why you are here.

When I ask you this and you tell me you are here for let us say a bump on your head. Then I ask you if you have recently injured and yourself and you tell me, "No, medial assistant Lori, I have not recently injured myself." I am typing all this information into your medical record. Then I ask you, "Are you here for any other complaints?" And you say, "No medical assistant Lori, it's only the bump on my head." Then I say, "Thank you, my beloved patient." And I head out of the room to get your favorite doctor. Guess what, I am going to tell them everything you just told me.

When your favorite doctor gets in the room, do not fucking lie to them and tell them that medical assistant Lori, never asked you if anything else, other than the bump on your head was wrong. Because this is what medical assistant Lori is going to tell your favorite doctor. "I guess your beloved patient is suffering from dementia or some other form of memory loss due to the bump on your fucking head." Asshole.

This is what happens when you tell the truth in the room when medical assistant Lori is in the room; when you tell me that you slammed your skull in the car door, yesterday and oh yea, this bruise on your elbow, is from when you rolled your car 3 weeks ago, and the hair in your left ear, that is driving you insane and that ingrown nail that is oozing green smelly pus should probably be looked at today, this is what I'm going to do, I'm going to tell your favorite doctor all this stuff you've just shared with me, you know why? Because when your favorite doctor gets in the exam room, he or she will not think they are only seeing you for one thing, when they are seeing you for six things! This makes the visit go much smoother for you, for me and for the doctor.

Medical Assistant Lori would also like to add that she does not appreciate it when she asks you why you are here and you tell me "A follow up," WTF. A follow up to what? And when I ask that, do not give me snotty attitude, and tell me to look it up in my iPad, because I am not going to. You are going to give me the fucking answer and if you do not, then I am going to go out and tell your doctor what a fuckstick you are.

I would also like to say that we would all really appreciate it, if you would wait to get undressed until we leave the room, especially if it is pertaining to a "sensitive area" I do not want to see that shit.

Men, please do not start taking off your clothes when we are in the exam room with you. That is so wrong in so many ways. Really, think about this. Ladies, same for you, honestly, I do not want to see any of anyone's parts or what is wrong with your parts, therefore I hate being the medical assistant. At the end of my day of being the stand in medical assistant, I leave the office with mental images, no one ever wants to have…. EVER.

Drapes & Gowns

All the medical assistants, including Medical Assistant Lori, will give you a drape or a gown for certain areas or procedures. If you tell us, you do not want one, then of course, we are not going to give you one, but do not dare tell your doctor we never offered you one. This is an unbelievably bad idea, because you see, I will remember who you are you little fuck and the next time you come in, I will only give you a corner of the drape or gown. Yeah, Karma is a bitch. Trust me I have a memory like an elephant.

If I am giving you a gown, I expect that you will follow my instructions to remove all your clothing and put the gown on. If you are the "C U Next Tuesday" that I recently saw that told me that, "you were not going to take off anything and that a full exam can be done on just your arms and legs", well I will try to be nice for a bit, before I leave the room and let your provider know all this. Then they can deal with your fucking bullshit.

To let you know, no "full" exam of any sort can be performed with your fucking clothes on Einstein. Or should I say, "Dr. Einstein." Fuck you, stupid mother fucker.

Sample Basket

This should be a simple one. First, and for most, it is a sample basket, i.e., small bottles of bigger bottles of stuff! If you do not know what samples look like, this may be a problem.

Samples are free, isn't that so nice? We are such a nice office, we want to give our patients nice free stuff, but do not rifle through the basket then find what you want, take fifteen things, and then ask if they are free. It is a God Damn sample. Samples are for your purse or your car, do not take fifteen of the goddamn things to fill your containers at home.

I always try to tell patients, it is kind a like trick or treating for adults, take one and move along. Quit being a greedy mother fucker and grabbing fifteen bottles of lotion, soap, or whatever, and then asking us for more. NO. You are not our only patient and we, do have other patients that would like a sample as well.

Also, please do not ask us if we have the Tide Samples or the Downy Samples, or the Dove Samples. We are not going to stop our day to reload the sample basket with what YOU like. You know why? Because its fucking free and we are not a God Damn grocery store. Jesus Christ.

Please do not ask us to check in the back. The back of what? It is not like we have a God Damn warehouse "in back of" the office full of samples. I do not understand what the reasoning is behind this thought. We do not have bays where the Tide and Downy Sample Truck comes and just unloads all their samples in the "back." WTF?!

Oh, and by the way, this basket is another source of income for us and will have you returning to us in no time flat. Think about that before you dip your hand into that stuff and start rifling through it!

Suckers or Lollipops

(Depending which state, you live in)

First, this is a major sore spot for me, I hate having to buy these stupid things for the office. One because I hate kids. This stems from working for a group of pediatricians for almost ten years. I pick up the trash from the suckers all over our fucking office, all fucking day long, all fucking year long.

The only thing, these suckers or lollipops are good for is generating more business for us.

Now I can see you thinking to yourself, "What?"

Let me explain, it is a major germ fest in that basket.

When I think of all the hands that are in that sucker basket or lollipop basket, it completely grosses me out. When I see boogery hands in there, hands with warts and God knows what else, I just laugh and think to myself, just drumming up more business for us and for the dentist next door!

Pens

Really, you are going to steal our pens?! By all means! Another infected item that will bring you right back to the office in no time flat! I simply love watching patients handle the pens at the check in and check out desks. Nothing gives me greater pleasure after I just watched someone put that pen in their mouth or ear, and you have just so secretly slipped it into your purse or pocket! And that is after the last twenty patients have handled the pen with genital warts and got knows what else! Wiped it all over their face, handled it with their rashy, warty, hands! We will see you in about ten days! Warts and cold sores are all viruses that just keep sharing the love via that lovely pen you just had to have!

You're welcome!

Vaping

I am sure about now, you are probably thinking to yourself, "WTF?" Yes, that was exactly what I was thinking when I had to tell you, the stupid patient, to quit vaping in our office.

Just a reminder you are in a doctor's office. When it is lunch time and I get called out of the kitchen, must put down my plate of food to go out to the waiting room and remind you where you are this is a sorry thing.

When you are that comfortable in our waiting room, I am truly scared for you. And yes, WHAT THE FUCK?! Your lame ass response is you forgot where you were? Again, WHAT THE FUCK? Are you honestly going to tell me your house looks like our waiting room? If this is the case, again, I am honestly scared for you, and you and your home must need some serious redecorating help.

Now for my employees that vape and think we just think someone shit cotton candy, grapes, and strawberries in the bathroom. We are not stupid. We know what you are doing in there and we want you to quit. Go outside with the rest of the Vapers, WTF.

Our Bathrooms

Are for our patients. End of story. Strangers and non-patient folk, please do not wonder into our office ask us if we have a bathroom, because this is a very stupid question. Although, I would like to tell everyone that asks me this, "No, we all wear Depends & shit ourselves all day long." Obviously we have a fucking bathroom.

Now for our patients, please do not come in to use our bathroom, knowing it has been seven days since you took your last crap, or that you feel a massive attack of diarrhea kicking in. As much as we want you to be comfortable during your exam there is a limit of how much of your stench we can take and how much the Hawaiian spray will cover up.

Also, bathroom etiquette comes into play here. Please do not piss on our floor or shit on the toilet seat. Do you do this in your own home? If you cannot wipe your ass, then you need to call someone to assist you, and preferably not one of us. Please bring a family member to the appointment that can wipe your ass.

It is bad enough that you have just destroyed our bathroom and now it smells like Hawaiian shitcicle in our hall. I would hate to see your damn underwear after this event.

The next patient has asked to use the bathroom and just informed the front desk that there is "pooh," "shit," "chunks," "crap," and everything in between on the seat and on the floor. "Wow, you've outdone yourself," Asshole.

Now it is my job to once again, don my favorite latex glove set and hope that the cleaning crew has left me something to clean with other than my fucking hands to clean your shit and piss off the floor. I am usually accompanied by a wonderful helper that I will refer to as Taylor, she is my right hand and hates to see me suffer alone and while we are taking turns gagging, the bathroom does manage to get cleaned and its ready for the next patient to have its way with, once again.

Undergarments

Ladies, please wear them. We all have tits, but we do not want to see yours in our face, nor do we want them resting on our front desk. Wear a bra. When I say this, I mean, do not wear a fluorescent orange bra and panties with a see-through white dress. It is not attractive when you weigh three hundred pounds. Your man may like it, but that is where it ends. Keep that shit at your house!

Men, please, please do not wear thong underwear or your silky, satin underwear when you are coming for a check on your man parts, or anything below your waste. We honestly are not interested in your underwear or your man parts, nor do we think it is hot or sexy. This totally applies to those in the age range of seventy- and eighty-year-old is, it applies to everyone.

Ladies, if you are coming for a procedure, let us say on your stomach and wearing a sun dress without underwear, do not look at us like a deer caught in headlights when we ask you to remove the dress. Then tell us in that innocent voice, "but I'm not wearing any underwear." Your choices are this, reschedule the appointment or take off the fucking dress. Lesson learned, we would all like to hope. Dumb shit.

By the way, who does this?!

Frankly and You People

Do not use these words when you are talking to us. I can tell you straight up, that if you talk to me using either one of these wording choices, I will turn it around so that you can hear just how stupid you sound speaking to me. Especially if you have used "frankly" ten times in one sentence, because quite "FRANKLY" if that is the only catch phrase you can come up with when you are speaking to me, then it is time for you to go back to school. After the fourth or fifth "frankly," you have lost my attention and I, FRANKLY, no long give two fucks about why you are complaining to me.

"You People." We are soooo NOT your people, and you can go fuck yourself when you start off any sentence or letter with that phrase. If you think for one milli-second, we are going to be nice and sweet to you after you start off with this, you are a fucking idiot.

Your ID and Insurance Card

You get an ID, let us say a state driver's license, which we all know as responsible adults we should carry on us if we drive or if we need to prove who we are. Right? Well, this is the same thought process for your insurance card.

Your insurance company prints up this little insurance card so that you can carry it with, let us say your driver's license and credit cards so when you go to the doctor or hospital, you can prove to all of us in the medical field that you have the insurance that you say you have.

What a brilliant concept.

Do not even try to come into the office without either one of these forms of identification. You will be turned away and your appointment will be rescheduled. Do not boo hoo to us that you have waited months for this appointment. That is bullshit. I know that we can get you an appointment within a day. I hate being lied to and it will just piss me off.

Also, do not try to tell us that your insurance company is no longer issuing cards, because this is what I will do. I will pull you in my office, call your insurance company and we will talk to them and ask them all about this, then we will reschedule your appointment, right after they tell me this is not true, and they will mail you a new fucking card.

When you come for your appointment and are asked for your ID and insurance card or cards at the front desk, we are going to scan them into our system as every other physician does on this planet these days. Do not stand there and argue with the front desk that you do not want your ID scanned into the system. You will be brought into my office and your ID, insurance card (s) WILL BE SCANNED INTO THE SYSTEM, or you can leave. If you tell me that you have not given me permission to scan your information into our computer system, the beauty of this is that I do not need your permission, this is how our office runs, if you do not like it, you can leave. It is really that easy.

Also, it would make our lives much easier if when we ask you for your identification or insurance card that you do not stand there and tell us it is in your wallet. So, what, take the fucking thing out and hand it to us or hand over your God Damn wallet, it's really that easy.

Patients with Tricare or a government issued ID. This applies to you too. Do not tell us we cannot scan your insurance cards into our system because it is a government ID, this is complete BULL SHIT, but then tell us its ok to take a copy of it and then destroy the copy, because here is what I am going to do. I am going to make a copy then when you leave, we are going to scan that nice copy we just made into your profile, just like we do with everyone else's shit.

Dental ID cards; do not present them to the front desk. We are not going to take them. You know why? Because we are a doctor's office, and we cannot help you with your fucking teeth. Do not try to tell us your dental card is the same as your health insurance card, it is not. Put it back in your purse or wallet, we are not interested in seeing it. Period. This also goes for your library card, grocery card or any other stupid card you try to present to us thinking it is your health insurance card. If it does not say "medical insurance" or "health insurance," it is not going to help you in our office.

Also, please do not show up for your appointment with twenty fucking insurance cards and expect us to figure out which one is active. We do not know. You know why? Because we do not carry the fucking insurance. You do!

Then when we do figure out what insurance you have, do not argue with us. We have just called all the phone numbers on all the cards you have given us. STFU and sit down.

Yelp

I hate you.

I hate the fact that Yelp representatives call and harass offices, like ours. Practically, daily, asking to speak to the doctors. Get real. It is never going to happen. You can leave ten thousand messages for them, and they are still never going to call you back. You know why? Because they are busy working being doctors! Do not call the office and pretend you are a patient, we have caller ID. Any call that comes from Yelp, gets re-directed to me. I know all the representatives there on a first name basis, which is how often you call us. When you get transferred to me and tell me how you can make our accounts with you "work for us," means nothing to me.

Yelp is a website for whiners, crybabies and motherfuckers that did not get their way, feel they can smear a good company or persons name or reputation by allowing people access to writing a shitty review and tell the rest of the cyber world just how terrible the place is they visited. Also note, it is always one sided. In my opinion, the website should rename itself to Cyber Crybabies Anonymous because that is all it is.

What truly drives me crazy about all this, is that the people that complain on Yelp and our Facebook page, complain, and then continue to come back for services. It is so funny that Yelp never gets to see that.

Patients that do not like the rules and when you are turned away because, you did not bring your ID, or your insurance card and you are a new patient, then you go straight away and post that we would not see you because you did not have any of the above are just showing the entire planet, how stupid you are. I really should thank you, because this is showing your insurance company that we really are doing our jobs and protecting ALL your medical information. Quit being a whining mother fucker and wake up.

Copays

If you have a copay at the time of your visit, we expect you to pay it at the time of your visit. Please do not tell us you do not have the money, you do not have your debit card, you do not have your wallet/purse, or you do not have your checkbook. We do not care. Your insurance company and every insurance company on the planet tells all doctor's offices that have a contract with your insurance that your copay is due at the time of service, and if you read your God Damn benefits book, you would know this. Copays are to be paid at the time of service. It irritates all of us that you cannot for whatever reason pay your five or fifty dollars at the time of service.

When you go to the grocery store, do you tell them you cannot pay? If you do, I can tell you that they are going to say, "tough shit, if you want your food, take out your money." It should not be any different at your doctor's office. When you go to the dentist, you *know* you are going to have to pay, this is a common knowledge thing. I cannot understand why, patient's just think that by telling us they are not going to pay is ok. Because in short, it is not.

Do not blame us for your copayment. How is this our fault? Every day we hear that your copay is so high, blah blah blah, poor me. Guess what dumbshit. You picked the plan, so this is on you!

Next, if you are the motherfucker patient that stood at my check out desk giving my check out girls a rash of shit, about how you should not have to pay your copay because it was a short appointment, we do not care. You had an appointment; you pay a copay. Then because you are a total douche bag, you file a grievance with your insurance company and tell your insurance company that you should not have to pay your copay because you had to wait thirty minutes for your appointment that was three minutes long, then you make another appointment for of all things a surgery!?

This is when I lose my shit and tell the surgeon, to please nick your artery and I will carry your dead ass carcass to the train tracks myself. FUCKING ASSHOLE. By the way we won that grievance and really appreciated you paying that forty-five-dollar copay in increments. How many stamps and envelopes did that cost you? Asshole.

Here is a little more information for you when you are complaining about your copay. On some if not many occasions the front/back desk girls will bring your insurance card to us or we will look up your insurance information on the website and present you with a printout from your insurance information, showing you that yes indeed, you are the lucky winner of a copay today! And with a little luck it is gonna be more than you thought! Bahahahahaha!

Now sometimes we do not know what your copay is and you as the patient play dumb. Some insurance plans have what is called a tiered program for copays and if this is your plan, then your copay can vary. It might look like this on your insurance card if you ever look at the bloody thing; 30/60/90.

We will more than likely take the middle tier and let you know after we take it, that your copay may indeed be the ninety dollar one. After we bill it out to your insurance and find out that your copay was ninety dollars, you will be billed for the thirty-dollar difference. Do not act like a fucker when you call to tell us we made a mistake on your copay, and you do not owe the thirty dollars. You do and it will sit on your account until you come back in.

No Shows

Asshole that you are, not only did you take up all our time scheduling the appointment over the phone but now you have chosen not to come to your appointment. Wow, just wow.

My favorite one, is calling us five minutes before your appointment to ask when your appointment is and acting like you have no idea and then canceling the appointment. When we all know that you made the appointment four days ago and two days ago, the automated system called or texted you to remind you of your appointment, but it is ok, go ahead and pretend like you do not know what the fuck is going on. We are going to tell you when you call us that this is also considered a "No Show."

Back in the old days when I worked for the pediatricians, we did not give warnings, if you did not show up, we just charged you twenty-five dollars and that was that. But that was also ten years ago, now it is 2019 and there is this thing called inflation or in laymen's terms, you have taken up our valuable time when we could be seeing someone who really needs to be seen, thanks for the dick move; and now we charge forty-five dollars.

Being that we are more civilized than you and we understand that life sometimes gets in the way of appointments, we now do not charge you for the first "No Show." You get a freebie on us, with a little warning per se, letting you know that if you do it again, you will indeed be charged the forty-five-dollar fee.

Now, I consider myself to be a fairly, nice and decent person, so do not be a fucker to me and call me up after you have received a bill for your "No Show" and act like you have no clue what this is for, when it clearly states on the bill what day you did not show up for.

Everything is documented, even the appointments you fail to show up for. Do not try to tell me, you did not come because it was a snow day, because you see, I keep track of all that.

On rare occasions, I may adjust off the fee, if you can prove to me that you have really had an emergency and truly could not make it to the office.

However, if I do this after you have whined to me about why you did not make the appointment and you make another appointment and do not show up for that one, then I will turn into an evil bitch and I will not give a fuck about one thing that has happened in your miserable life. Oh, and you will be charged the forty-five-dollar fee and then you cannot make another appointment until you pay the fee. Honestly, nothing makes me happier than knowing this.

My most favorite excuse for people not showing up, is because they did not make the appointment. When you call me to argue with me about your "No Show" fee and you tell me that you did not call and make the appointment, but your referring physician did, that is one thing.

Do not call and tell me that our computer system just made the appointment for you randomly. I cannot tell you how many times I hear this. Our computer system does not make appointments for random people. In fact, our computer system cannot make appointments at all without someone inputting the information into the system.

 This is the most idiotic thing I have ever heard come out of patient's mouths. I really want you think about this before you say something this stupid. I also hear from you that we are just making random appointments for people to fill our schedules. Oh, My Fucking God, are you kidding me? And then charging you the innocent patients to increase our revenue. This is downright hilarious! Forty-five dollars is going to increase our revenue only if you pay it and most of you do not.

Also, please do not call and try to tell me you are a long-time patient. I do not care. That is awesome and means absolutely nothing to me. While you are telling me, you are a long-time patient and are appalled by us charging you the "No Show" fee, just means that you think you are once again better than the rest of us and from the Land of Entitlement and this my friend does not work for me and never will. You will pay the fee every mother fucking time.

The Elevator Does Not Work and more

This section is for people that aren't our patients and just randomly wander into our office to tell us stupid shit, like the elevator doesn't work Or there is a giant icicle hanging from the roof, there is a dead bird on the lawn, why is the parking attendant not in his booth, the front door isn't working, someone hit a car in the parking lot and left, there is a lady that can't walk up the stairs, there is a lost woman in the building, the sidewalks have ice on them, it smells like gas in the building, why isn't there a mailbox in the building, why isn't there an ATM in the building, there is a strange man in the parking lot, a man locked his keys in his truck, why are the police parked in the parking lot, ICE agents are pulling a little girl out of a car on the street. There is someone sleeping on the hill across the street, "do you think she's dead?"

There is a lady in the parking lot asking patients for money and knocking on their car windows asking for cash? Now how is this my problem? Do I look like I work for building management?

The list goes on and guess what, we do not care, you know why, because we are working and are oblivious to what is going on outside. Please do not come to our office to tell us this stupid shit. What makes you all think that we can fix all this shit? Or that we want too?

The Directory

Please use it.

I cannot tell you how many times patients come into our office with their lab paperwork and tell us in front of all our waiting room patients, they are here for a "piss test". So awesome. It does not seem to matter if our suite was on the first floor or third floor, people just wander around aimlessly, when on the very first floor when you walk in any building, there is a directory that tells you exactly where your doctor or lab is.

In fact, in our building the directory is the size of the fucking wall. I am not sure how everyone is missing it unless, you are all blind or something.

If you do not know who your doctor is or who you made the appointment with, then you have a problem. Please do not come into our office and think we are going to solve your problem. Then when we cannot, give us attitude. That does not work for us, and you will be asked to leave, or I will personally escort you out of the office myself.

I find that patients just come into our office and say they are here for their appointment and after the front desk wastes their time trying to check you in, only to find out that you are not our patient, this is infuriating. Why you ask? Well, because right on our front door it says what office it is. If you are supposed to be seeing an ear doctor, then do not walk into the cardiologist and tell them you have an appointment! For these people this is when I just want to mouth the words, so they cannot hear them, then send them upstairs thinking they cannot hear. Yes, it is the evil bitch in me.

Quest or LabCorp

Again, not only is the directory on the ginormous fucking wall when you walk in, but they also have a sign in the middle of the God Damn lobby that says, "Quest Lab is downstairs". Please do not show us how stupid you are by coming into our office and asking us, "Where is Quest Laboratory?" Then ask us after we tell you it is downstairs, how to get there. You are kidding me, right? This is the point where I want to come out of my office aim you in the direction of the stairs and kick your sorry ass down them. There is also this wonderful invention called an elevator, it will also take your stupid ass down there. It would also be amazing if you would quit asking us what their office hours are. Let me tell you, we do not fucking know; we do not fucking care and there is a mother fucking sign in the middle of the fucking lobby telling you where it is and what the hours are! If you cannot figure out how to get down there, this is your problem.

Products

Most physician offices these days, sell some sort of products to their patient. I know an eye doctor that sells, vitamins, and of all things does Botox. We are a specialist, and we sell all sorts of skin care products. Anyone can buy them, not just our patients. But if you are going to be an asshat and come in to buy product, when we ask you your name, just give us your fucking name. Do not tell us you are not going to give us that "personal information" as we do not need it then give us your fucking credit card to pay. You are a fucking moron.

We collect state tax on all the products we sell, do not stand at my back desk, and argue with my girls and tell them it is against the law for us to collect tax, what the fuck? I am going to come out of my office and not happy, mind you and tell you that the state tells us we must collect tax, then I am going to give you the phone number for the state taxation department, and you can call and bitch at them. You can either buy our products or not. If you think for one second, we are in the business of selling products and making a killing off this you are sadly mistaken, we do this as a courtesy to patients, so people with certain needs have better products accessible to them.

Returning Product

Please do not expect that after you have used nearly eighty percent of the bottle that you are going to come in and get another one for free. This is sheer idiotic.

Also, do not bring product in after you have had for a year or two and expect a full refund, it will never happen. Products change and so do the lines that we carry. You will get a refund, but it is not going to be for the price you paid, especially if it has been a year or two. Honestly, the only time we are ever supposed to exchange anything is if you are allergic to it or the bottle is defective. What this means is do not hold onto it for three years, tell us you had an allergic reaction to it after you used eighty percent of it and now, you would like your money back, the answer will be no.

Prescriptions

Prescriptions are no longer called in. Everything currently is done electronically. Gone are the days when the doctor would just write out a prescription on a prescription pad and hand it to the patient. It is exceedingly rare that my physicians whip out that pad anymore. Kind of makes me sad, but it is a much more efficient and cuts down on us hearing, "I lost my prescription".

Let us talk a little more about your prescriptions. Do not call us for a refill on your prescription when you knowingly have not been in the office in six years. The answer will always be no and will never be yes. Best to quit the whining and just make the appointment. Also, do not try to call back after we tell you, "No," and try to ask for a different physician to fill it. We are not stupid.

Please do not call and ask for the prescription of, "that lotion" that you got three years ago, or "the football shaped pills." What the fuck? Do you not know what the fuck you are taking? This literally drives me crazy. Then you expect us to go through your entire medical chart to find what dose you are on. This does NOT work for us. In short, when you call for your prescription, know what the fuck medication and dosage you are taking.

Yes, we have the answers in your chart, but the people that answer the phones do not have all day to look at your medical records and try to figure out what you were prescribed three years ago, nor do they know the shape and color of your God Damn pills. Even better, how 'bout calling your pharmacy? What a concept. They could call us or fax us. That is the new thing these days, then we can tell them No and they will tell you No.

On another note, when you are calling in a prescription refill for yourself, and Medical Assistant Lori calls you back for more information, for instance to ask you what the fuck prescription you want, please do not tell me it is that tube of white cream and really your brother uses it more than you do but you still need a refill on it. This is never a good idea to admit.

When you do call your doctor's office and you must leave a message on the voice mail, do not just say, "Hi this is Mary and I need a refill on my prescription call it into CVS." Then hang up. Hello tardo! We can't call you back without your last name, date of birth or how 'bout this your fucking phone number. Then when we do not call you back, do not call and be a fucker to us because we did not call you back, because you see, I will be the first one to let you know that you, idiot Mary, did not leave us any information and I will recite the idiotic message we received from you. Honestly, why can't you just use your fucking brains?

Prescription Prior Authorizations

Nothing is simple in the insurance world with prescriptions. Medications now require prior authorizations.

Meaning, your insurance company gets to decide whether they are going to pay for your prescriptions or not. This does not mean that every prescription needs a prior authorization, it just means that some drugs on your plan may need one.

Please do not get pissy with us, if your prescription needs an PA (Prior Auth) - honestly, it is more work for us and if you are going to be a prick about having to wait, then we will just take our sweet old time getting you one. Please also note, this is something the insurance company has set up, we are just following their rules. Do not call us six times a day and be a dick to us, when you should be calling your insurance company and being a dick to them. The squeaky wheel will not always get the oil in this case. Some things take time, and this is just one of those things.

I would also like to add that we really do try hard to get PA's, but it is very time consuming, and most end up being denied. Let me add that the amount of paperwork and time that go into a medication prior authorization is incredible and migraine worthy.

Please make sure this is something you really want because after we finally get the approval and I get the lovely task of calling you to tell you it has been approved but your copay is seven hundred dollars, it kills me to hear, "Well I'm not going to pay that, you can tell my doctor, I need a different prescription." This is just about the time, when I am going to pull you through the phone cord and watch the phone come out your asshole, because it has taken me fifteen days to get approval on this God Damn thing.

Oh, and all the drug commercials on tv for all the injections and what not make me think of my beloved patients, with a syringe in your head. That is right and I put it there. Can you say Voodoo Doll? I can.

Walk-ins

Do not walk into the office and expect on a Monday morning that you are going to get worked into the schedule. In fact, do not think this any day. People make appointments for a reason. Not only will it piss off the people that have appointments, but it pisses us off as well. If you are having a true emergency, this is where an urgent care comes into play or the emergency room or a fucking ambulance!

Just because you were camping on a red ant hill last weekend, and you want to explain to the front desk about every orifice of your body has ant bites on it, or worse want to show us, in front of a waiting room full of patients this is not our problem. I would like to think I am a compassionate person, but my sympathy river has dried up over the years and now the I do not give a fuck river is overflowing. Call the office and make an appointment like everyone else or go to urgent care.

Minors with appointments

If your child is not eighteen, they cannot come to the office and be a patient by themselves. You know why? Because they are not a fucking adult! HELLO! Do not just drop off your child off at the office and think we are going to see them without their mommy or daddy. We need a note from you, the parent, saying it is ok for them to be "treated." You know why? Because children that are sixteen and seventeen years old cannot make an informed decision on anything let alone their health care and need their mommies and daddies for this.

Then when we see them without you and we treat them for let us say a wart, you as the mommy or daddy cannot come back on us after your stupid kid that wanted his wart burned off and tell us you did not authorize this.

Also note, that your child can fill out the form, but they cannot sign it, because they are not a fucking adult so do not call us or be a fucker to us when we ask you, the mommy or daddy to sign the form the next time you come in with your kid.

Next let us address sending your child with grandma or whomever. If they come with anyone other than you, they need a note from you. That is how it is. Do not be a fucker to us, whining or bitching at us will get you know where. You MUST be available by either phone or have the note that says we can "treat your child," otherwise we are only going to see them, we are not going to do anything to them. Then they will have to make another appointment and yes, pay another copayment, and come in and be "treated." This is also applying to sending your kids with your other kids. Do not send your fourteen-year-old with your seventeen-year-old. We will not be able to see your child, they must be with a responsible adult.

Follow Up Appointments

Follow up appointments are an appointment. Plain and simple. If you walk into any physician's office and have an office visit, it is an office visit. There for, we will collect a copay. Do not try to tell us this "is a follow up appointment" we know, and you still owe a copay. Even better, do not call us to argue with us after the fact, we will tell you, you still had an office visit, because you did. The only time a copay does not apply is after a surgery. So, if you want to get sliced and diced on and not have a copay, this is your only option. Do not try to tell us we are raping you for your copays. Call your fucking insurance company. That is on them and you, since you are the one that chose the plan. Do not try to blame us. We do not care.

Bat Shit Crazy

If this, is you, please do not call us

End of chapter.

The Full Moon

This is a legit thing. Anyone in law enforcement or in the healthcare industry utterly understands the moon cycles and does not look forward to the full moon at all. Why, you ask? Well, Bat Shit Crazy people come out of their caves, and it usually lasts for a week, sometimes two, and it is usually stuff you just cannot make up. For instance, wanting to make an appointment with us because you have a stomachache, we cannot help you, but your primary care physician can. Call them. Or wanting to know if we sell rubber gloves... I don't even have a response for this one.

Lost and Found

Lost and found, this is an interesting topic. We do not really have one. If you lose something in our office and we find it and we know it is yours, we will call you. If we do not know it is yours, we will either hold it for a while or we will put it on our front desk, like the Elsa doll and wait for someone to claim it. Now here is where you, the patient come into play on all this. If the office calls you and says, "Hello, Mr. Doe, we found your credit card today." Please come to the office to get your lost Visa, do not send your third cousin twice removed to come get it. We will not give it to them. We will only give it to you after we see your ID and you prove to us that it is really you! Now if it is just a pair of sunglasses or an umbrella or something like that, we will hold it for a while and then if no one calls for it, we will auction it off to the employees or we will simply just throw it away. Calling three months after the fact to say, you are calling for your lost umbrella is a bad idea. We do not have it anymore.

Millennials

This is a term for bad parenting. In short you as parents, did not do your jobs and just raised a bunch of fucking brats and now we as professionals must deal with your poor choices.

That is right; a generation of little fuckers that used to be five and six years old but are now twenty-five and twenty-six years old and act like they are five or six. Also, I would like to add the, some thirty-year old's fall into this category as well. Grow up.

That does not mean every one that is in their twenties or thirties acts like a fucking brat, it just means that most of you are giving a bad name to the rest of your gang. The rest of us that have grown up are done with your shit.

Aides

When you bring your patient or patients to our office, let's make sure of a couple of things; one, you're in the right office, two, you have control over your patients and three, they don't need to pee....When I say this it's because yes you, the man that had not one but four handicapped men that came into our office while I was handing out paychecks and hearing my front desk supervisor scream, "Jesus Christ, he doesn't have any pants on!" And then my lead medical assistant screaming, "He can't pee in our bathroom!!" Then I am turning around to see a man with yes, no pants on, big floppy penis, swinging in the wind while his aide and the other incapacitated patient of his, chase after this man. Trust me, this is something that you cannot unsee and never goes away. I know what you are going to ask, "Did we have patients?" Well of course we did! In the waiting room where he unrobed and coming out of the exam rooms, and yes, I did let him pee in our bathroom instead of the patient bathroom, because if I did not, he would have pissed all over the hallway and honestly, I was not up for cleaning up that! Oh, and after this fiasco, he was walked back to the waiting room, obviously relieved, without his pants on, I mean why not, we have already seen everything. I guess no one thought to get his pants and bring them to the bathroom, but in my staff's defense, the other two handicapped gentlemen were left to roam the waiting room by themselves, and they were completely out of control, leaning over the front desk counter, and taking my staffs breakfast, drinks, pens and whatever they could get their hands on. In front of our most gracious patients. After all this, the aide returns to the waiting room with our streaker only to ask, "Where is the lab?" Are you fucking kidding me? You are a fucking asshole.

So, you are a Doctor, Now

I am just wondering where you received your medical degree from. I am wondering because you have just called me to tell me that your doctor should have done surgery on you. I find your opinion interesting.

 No, I do not, that is a fucking lie!

 It always intrigues me to hear that you came in and the doctor should have done this or that to you. Based on what, is what I would like to ask. But you are usually screaming at me, and I cannot get a word in edgewise. Here is the beauty of this, when you are in the room, having your visit, you the patient get to speak with your doctor. I know right, you can open your fucking mouth and speak. If you do not, well that is on you. Do not call me after the fact to tell me that whatever is wrong with you is still wrong with you and you should have had this or that done. The only way I can help you is by making another appointment for you and collecting another copay – which by the way, is something else, I live for.

Surgery Consults

If you need to have a surgery, you must have a surgery or surgical consult. Do not try calling in and just making a surgery appointment. Every scheduler in the office knows that patients need a consult. In fact, every employee in the office knows this. No one can simply come in for surgery. Do not lie to us and tell us that you have had your consult. We will look it up in your medical records to check while you are on the phone and you will not be happy with the appointment, we choose for you.

The surgeon needs to see you to assess your case before he cuts you open. I really need you to think of a surgeon who does not see his patient before going into surgery. This does not apply to surgeons in the emergency room, because they have seen it all already, they are just waiting for your ass to show up so they can fix something.

General surgeons who see patients in the office and then do surgery on their patients always do a consult first. So, they can put your mind at ease and answer all your stupid ass questions, that you never listen to the answer anyways then call us on a holiday weekend to tell us that you are bleeding profusely from wherever and now what you are supposed to do.

Please do not come into our office as a new patient thinking you are the doctor, you are not. You still need to see a provider, have them assess your case, then after you are examined, and only then, will you be told you need to see the surgeon for a consult.

Do not for one fucking second think that it gets you a free pass to surgery, it does not. Also do not call the office after you have received your bill to tell me that you should have been scheduled with the surgeon to begin with. YOU are given a choice of who you want the appointment with when you make the fucking appointment. If you take an appointment with a Nurse Practitioner and she says you must see the surgeon for a consult, you will now have two or three copays. Do not call us telling me, you little fuck millennial, that you were only expecting two copays. This is about the time; I welcome you into adulthood.

Surgery patients are always sent home with directions, do not try to tell us you did not get directions, because you see, it is all notated in your medical records.

24 Hour & Weekend Coverage
Emergencies Only

All doctor offices have twenty-four-hour coverage for emergencies. Please do not call the physician on call in the middle of a snowstorm to say you need a refill on your prescription when you have known for three days that a blizzard is coming. At this point, we are thinking a few things, one, WTF, two, no, three, this is not an emergency and four you are a true idiot.

I would also like to remind everyone of what a true emergency is. You are bleeding, your stitches are oozing some gross shit, your surgery site is inflamed, red and swollen, you have a rash over your entire body, and you have now swelled up to the size of the Stay Puft Marshmallow Man, part of the nerf football is up your kid's nose, there is a bean in my kid's nose, there is a barbie shoe in my kid's nose (those are my favorites). If you call for any other stupid shit you are going to be told to call the office on Monday. Then when you call us on Monday, do not tell us you talked to "that guy" or "that girl." That guy and that girl would be the fucking doctor, dickwad.

Medical Records

Medical Records are the property of the office. Do not call me and tell me they belong to you, because they do not. They belong to us. If you would like a copy of them, we would love to give you one for the mere price of Twenty-five dollars. Now here is where the whining starts. "Twenty-five dollars, which is ridiculous!" Honestly, it is not. We must copy them and not only does that take my employee's time, but it also takes my paper, and it takes my toner. Twenty-Five dollars is very fair. Here is the super deal of the day, if you just want them faxed to your doctor, it is free! Please do not tell me we are just trying to rape you, because if we were raping you, we would sure as shit be charging more than twenty-five dollars for records.

You must also sign for your medical records to be sent to where you would like them to go. Some records I would like to send to hell, because most of you have come from there, but that is another story all together. Anyway, please do not give me any grief about this, just send a signed note, with your date of birth and where you want them sent. Do not try to just email me some bullshit note with a typed name on it as your signature, this is not going to work.

Also, please do not even think by telling me you either work in the medical field or work for a doctor that this is beyond your comprehension that we make you pay for your records or your children's records or anyone in your family's records. Also do not tell me that "your doctor" doesn't charge for records, because in short, I don't give a fuck what "your doctor's office" is doing. This is our policy and if you want the records mailed or faxed to you, then you will pay for them. Do not try to tell me that you will send payment after you receive the records. Wrong answer. The way this works is that you will pay for your records prior to them ever leaving "the office."

Asshole.

As a side note on this, you should also be aware of, if you owe the office money, we consider that part of your medical records as well, and that information will also be forwarded to your new physician. I mean we should let them know that you did not want to pay your services with us so why would you want to pay for services with them...

Pictures

Pictures are part of your medical record. We ask to take a picture of you, so that we can identify you. Please do not pose for your picture. We just want to see your face.

It is not a glamour shot or your high school senior picture. Jesus, just sit there and look forward into the damn camera lens. We also take pictures of your issues, no matter where they are. This is just a heads up. So, if you say you have an inflamed penis, then Mr. Unhappy will be having his picture taken, it will of course be a head shot!

Free Office Visits

I get a lot of phone calls on this one.   We do not offer services for "free" in our office. You know why? Because it is not a Free Clinic. Please do not call the office after you have had a visit, received your bill, do not like your bill and try to tell me that it was for a free visit. We do not have free visits in fact nothing in life is free except Herpes, but you will end up paying for that in the end somehow too. Eeek

Statements

God, please do not call us and tell us you do not know why we are sending you a statement. It says right on there what it is for. Then when we tell you what it is for, do not tell us you did not come in that day. Here is what is going to happen, we are going to look up in your medical records, see that you were here, then go and look in our other system where we scan all the paperwork that you sign on that day and tell you, that you were here. Do not be a fucker to us and tell us you are turning us into your insurance company, because right here is where I am going to tell you, "Bring it on."

Then when your insurance company calls us, we are going to send all our shit to them and prove to them that yes, indeed you came, asshole and signed the form saying we could file the claim and that you would pay any outstanding amounts owed. Quit wasting our time and just pay your God Damn bill.

 Two copays in one day, well it happens, do not blame this on us, call your shitty insurance company, in fact, call your insurance company first, they are the ones that tell us what they are paying and what they are not paying. We do not make this shit up on our own.

Guess what, you as the patient, get what is called an Explanation of Benefits or EOB from your insurance company about ten days before we send you a bill. It tells you just what we are going to send you a bill for. Isn't that neat?

"Is this a real statement?" Yes, we do not send fake ones. What the Fuck.

"I never received a statement." Bullshit. We keep track of what we send out to you. We also keep track of returned mail and if we do not get any mail back, then the statement was delivered to you. Do not call me and tell me you NEVER received one, especially after we have sent six. My response will be that I do not work for the post office and may I suggest calling them.

"Can you mail me out another statement?" Let me see. NO. If you have had two statements already, that tells me that in the last sixty days you had no intention of paying us and by wasting my time, paper, toner, envelope, and stamp, you still have no intention of paying us. There for, you will be asked to pay while you are either standing in front of us or on the phone.

If you tell me that you are not going to pay, then you are not going to come back. EVER.

Notes on The Statement

This is entertainment for us. When you write a shitty note on the statement and send it back to us with your payment, we just laugh and laugh and laugh. What the Fuck ever. Mostly, we get, "you are thieves" "I'm never coming back," "this cost is not justifiable," "you guys charge too much", "this is highway robbery, send an envelope and you'll get my money faster," the list goes on. We laugh because, you are not the doctor. If you do not want to pay the amount listed on the statement, get better fucking insurance or go to medical school, become a doctor and treat yourself. Asswipe.

Envelopes

You are mad because we do not send envelopes with your statement. Well, the reason why we do not, is because we do not have to. If you would like us to send an envelope with your statement this is only going to drive up costs of your office visit. When you write this stupid shit on your statement that you want us to send you a God Damn envelope think of us raising our prices, which by the way has not happened in nearly ten years.

Forms of Payment

Honestly, we will take just about any form of payment. We take all major credit cards, even Care Credit. We will take checks, (see next chapter about exclusions), cash and we will even take your pennies. Please do not send cash in the mail, why would you do this? If this is really what you are going to do, can you at least just bring it into the office. Mailing it is just so stupid and moronic.

Care Credit: this is a credit card that helps you out and we at the doctor's office really do not like it but for the good of the patients take it anyways. The reason is because it is a total pain in the ass for us. I am only speaking for me and my office, but I am sure I am not alone when I say this. Care Credit is offered as a form of payment in our office but beware, that we will only finance your services for six months. Meaning that if you pay it off in six months, then there is no interest, if you choose not to pay it off in six months, then they are going to charge you out the ass and put on their interest which is something like twenty-five to twenty-six percent of the amount charged. We will only take it if your services are over fifty dollars. Do not be fuckers to us and tell us we are not helping you out at all. Also note that we as physicians or dentists that offer this to our patient must take a discount on your services. Yeah, super special. Another reason why we hate it. Your other option is to just use your regular credit card and get totally raped for the annual percentage rate they offer. And this is just what I will tell you when you come in my office and tell me that you do not like the deal.

Credit Card Payments when you send us a credit card payment in the mail. You must write it on the part of the statement that you are sending back. There is an actual spot on the top part of the statement for your credit card number. This is a brilliant concept. Do not send us the bottom of your statement that has no identifying items on it, sign your name illegibly and not write your credit card number on it. Who does this stupid shit?

If you are the person that keeps doing this, you are not paying your bill, you are just wasting your stamps and your own fucking envelope that you have bitched at us for not sending you one of ours! Quit doing this!

If you are the person that sends us your credit card but only sends us a partial number, this is a problem. We will try to call you, and we will even leave you a message if you do not answer. Do not expect us to keep calling you. We will scan that lovely part of the statement into your account and when you call to tell us you have paid your bill already, after we have sent you another statement, we can have a lovely conversation about how did not give us the entire credit card number. We will both laugh about it and then hang up and run your card while we are muttering what a dumb ass you are.

Checks (Exclusions)

You want to write the office a check. That is great, we take checks, but if you bounce that check, here is where the exclusion comes in. First, we will charge you a returned check fee or NSF (non-sufficient funds) fee. Twenty to Thirty-five dollars, it will depend on what the bank charges us, plus whatever the amount of check was. Then you can no longer write the office checks. Please do not whine to me that it is all your bank's fault and not yours. I do not care. Cash and or credit cards are your friends now if you choose to return to the offices for services.

If you write a check for seven hundred or so and it bounces, then we have a bigger problem. Of course, the same fees apply but if you choose to ignore my phone calls on this, then you have forced me to call the police.

This is when writing a bad check turns into larceny or a felony, which tends to be a crime. It also is a big pain in the ass for me, because there is a ton of paperwork to file with the police and the court.

After the police are notified and they come to take my statement and I supply them with ALL the paperwork on this. Then police will call you, if you choose not to answer them, then they will have no choice but to put out a warrant for your arrest.

Before the warrant is issued, I will call you one more time to see if we can square up your little issue of non-payment for services rendered. I will be nice and leave you a cryptic message, letting you know if the debt is not paid then you cannot come back to the office. The account will be flagged as a "LARCENY ACCOUNT." Of course, I cannot say hardly any of this because I cannot leave a message that someone else might overhear letting them know you are now a larcenist. So, I ever so nicely ask you to call the office regarding your check number whatever 3232 for example.

If I do not hear from you in three business days, then I call the police again and the warrant will be issued. Then we just play the waiting game. I am great at playing this game. Nothing makes me happier knowing there is a warrant out for your arrest. You will be arrested the next time you are caught speeding or something lame like that and all I can envision is you in handcuffs wondering WTF and cursing me! It really does make my day!

After you are arrested, the District Attorney calls us. It is usually six months to a year that this happens, but still it happens. After we speak with the DA it is time to make a deal. We unlike you, are not Mother Fuckers. We just want our money. You will only be asked to pay what you owe us, which by the way is a fair deal.

We will even let you pay through the court in increments. But have no fear, I will have the name, phone number and email of your new best friend...Your Parole Officer.

 Now if it is just a bad check of up to, two hundred and fifty dollars, then I will just file a small claim against you. This is also a monster pain in the ass, but let me assure you, I do not care how much paperwork it is, I will do it. I also NEVER miss a court date and I ALWAYS show up. What is also interesting is that when I provide all your medical records to the court, they become public record until either you or I pick them up. Trust me on this. After I win, I am not going back for your medical records.

If you do not show up for your court date, then the court issues a warrant for your arrest, and we wait. As previously stated, I have no problem waiting. The waiting games is one of my most favorite games to play. FUCKERS.

Collections

If you do not pay, you do not play.

Your account is sent to our in-house collections. We send you a letter to the same lovely address where your statements are sent. You know, the ones you never get but the post office never sends back to us. We monitor these accounts. There are big red flags on these accounts for when patients call, you will be immediately put on hold and transferred into the billing office, where you will be told that in order to make an appointment you must pay the balance of your account. Now do not sound shocked, when we tell you, that you have a balance from 2015.

May I also say that we are doing you a favor by not sending the account to a real collection agency and just keeping the account in house, just waiting for you to call us for an appointment.

To the cow that called me and was screaming at me because I would not write off your balance from 2015. You owe it. I know this because your insurance says you do. Do not tell me that six years ago you did not give us the insurance we have on file. Bullshit. We do not randomly just put insurance on patients accounts then bill them out. The information came from somewhere and rest assured we did not provide it. You did. You are telling me that you never received a statement from us at this point, all I am hearing is blah blah blah blah blah. Again, two if not three statements were sent, sometimes we have even been known to send six statements and still you do not pay.

I do not care that you think you did not get them. Can you really remember getting a statement from us six years ago, because if you can, I would like to know, why you did not call us then, you stupid bitch.

Sometimes, my employees do not see the big red flags that say, "COLLECTIONS ACCOUNT", and make you an appointment anyways, you will get a phone call asking you to call the office prior to your appointment, if you do not call, you will have a big surprise waiting for you when you come in for your appointment....ME.

The Doctor's Jag or Mercedes

When you tell me after we have talked about your bill and you tell me that, we are making you pay this "outrageous amount" so the doctor can buy his/her Jag or Mercedes. You really have no clue. All the physicians I ever worked for all had regular cars. Jaguars and Mercedes must be for the cardio-vascular surgeons or the anesthesiologist to drive because from my experience the providers I work for are not driving these.

Furthermore, the amount we charge you is not the amount we get paid. There are adjustments made on the account and your copay, which all you mother fuckers bitch about paying, or feel you never need to pay.

New Patient Visit

VS

Established Patient Visit

You would think this would be the easiest thing in the world to understand but for some reason, patients are just not getting this.

If you are a new patient, we charge a new patient visit, meaning it is going to cost you more because you are a NEW Patient and you have never been to the office. We don't' know you, there's more to the visit.

If you are an established patient, there are many types of OFFICE visits the providers can choose to bill you. Ranging from minimal to quite detailed. This part should be easy to understand. If it is a minimal visit, it is going to be cheaper than the more detailed visit.

Now if you are an established patient and you have not come to see us in three or more years then you are considered a "NEW" patient. Do not try to tell me that we cannot do this. We can, we do, and even more fantastic is that all insurances are okay with this! It is a magical time for us!

Procedures vs Office Visits

Procedures are not considered to be office visits. You may have an office visit where a procedure is done but it is not one and the same. In fact, your insurance may charge you two copays, and yes this is something that your insurance does do.

An office visit is when you come to see us, and we just look at something on your body. No treatment is rendered.

A procedure is when we cut off your head and send it to the lab as a specimen. Secretly, I hope this will happen, and it saddens me when it does not.

Referrals

Here it is, patients, if you need to have a referral to go to a specialist, your primary care physician (PCP) needs to do a referral. If you do not know what this is or have no idea what your insurance benefits are, this is a problem. What is also a problem is that, it is not your PCP's issue to do the referral and it is not our problem to do the referral. if they do not know you are going to see a specialist. You physically must call them and request a referral. If you do not do this, you will be asked to sign a waiver when you come in for your appointment with the specialist. Do not act all the surprised when the front desk girls ask you if you have your referral. "Huh, what's that?" "I've never had to get one of those before," yeah, we know, blah blah blah, blah blah, yet you have had this insurance for the past ten years, mind boggling. "This must be something new my insurance is doing." No, it is not, read your fucking policy. Its on-line, I can give you the web address.

Another tid-bit of information is we know which insurances need referrals and which ones do not, and since we are so nice and we want to get paid, we do a little (really a lot) of extra work for our beloved patients and send a fax on your behalf to your primary care physician, asking them to do the referral so you will not be caught having to pay for the visit. Do not come in and be assholes to us if you need a referral.

The Waiver

If you do not sign it, you are not going to be seen. It is just like all the other forms. Do not try to change it, you will be given a new one. Do not ask us what it says, you need to read it and sign it. It says you will be responsible for the visit if you do not get a referral from your primary care physician, then you sign it. Really this is one of my favorite forms, because when you do not get your referral and your insurance does not pay for your visit, you get a bill from us. And nothing makes me happier than a phone call from you wanting to know why we are billing you four hundred dollars for an office visit! It also makes me happy to tell you that you signed the waiver.

Now do not call your insurance company and tell on us, because we are going to tell them you signed a waiver, knowing you neglected to tell them that in your conversation. We usually just email it or fax it to them and then let them call you back with the fantastic news that you owe us the four hundred dollars.

There are times when we forget to have the waiver signed, five hundred patients checking in at one time, phones ringing off the hook, copy machine jammed, providers looking for lab results and just general chaos. Not to worry though, at the very end of your demographic form that you fill out, it says right on there that you give your permission for us to bill your insurance, (that's why you sign the form by the way) and that if your insurance does not pay then you are responsible for any balances that are incurred. On the off chance that we really don't get the waiver form signed we are fucked. We will not get paid by your insurance without a referral if one is not obtained. We cannot bill you, the patient. This pisses me off. It rarely happens because of the fantastic staff I employ but it does happen.

Medicaid

This is a touchy subject. I think most patients that are on state mandated insurance really do need it. Then there are those that are scamming the system. This irritates us all. If you even try for one second to deny this, you are a lying mother fucker. Not only are you lying to the rest of us, but you are also lying to yourself.

I usually do not have an issue with people or patients on Medicaid, until I see that they have better benefits than I have. Then I fucking lose my shit! The reason, well in short, I work my ass off for my benefits, the ones that I MUST pay for, then every state in America fucks all of us working fold and makes all of us pay the benefits of the needy, or uninsured, and this does not sit well with me. What also does not sit well with me, is Medicaid patients, I find are the most demanding, rude, and ungrateful patients on the planet. Fuck you guys.

For whatever reason, you all seem to think you are entitled to these benefits that you do not pay for, then you come into the office and treat us all like shit, forgetting that all the working people of America are paying for YOUR fucking benefits. The people behind the desk checking you in, the doctors and nurses taking care of you. Everyone in our office is paying your state mandated insurance, you need to be nice and bring your fucking card, like we have asked you too.

Of course, this is not for all Medicaid patients, because let us be honest, maybe ten percent of the Medicaid crowd are grateful for the benefits and are the nicest people to speak to, but the rest of you bastards can fuck off.

Medicaid patients need referrals from the PCP's or primary care physician to go see a specialist. Do not call us and be a total fucker when we tell you this, after you have been on Medicaid for five years. You KNOW this. Medicaid patients cannot even make an appointment without having a referral on file. The reason for this is because Medicaid will not pay us for your visit. That means, after we charge the state for your visit, they will not pay us the six dollars. I know most of you do not give a rat's ass about this as you have blatantly said so, and most, if not all of you think we should just give you the health care for free, and I am not sure why you think this but again you can just go fuck yourselves.

What also drives us insane about Medicaid patients, is when they ask if they can just pay out of pocket for their visit. Ummm NO WTF. If you can pay for your God Damn visit out of pocket, i.e., in cash, then WTF are you doing on state mandated insurance. This is really a bad thing to ask us, and we will tell you NO, because we could lose our contract and even worse you could lose your Medicaid benefits, you know the benefits you just demonstrated to us that you don't need. WTF? WTF?

Referrals

I know you may not know this, but we verify your insurance the day before you come into the office for your exam. We do this for three reasons; one, to make sure you do have the insurance policy you say you have, two, so we get paid, and three and most important, so you do not have to pay. Do not be fuckers to us when we call you the day before your appointment to tell you we have bad insurance on file or the policy we have has termed. We are doing you a fucking favor!!! Do not tell me that we should be verifying your insurance a week in advance! Get a fucking grip on your bad self, asshole. Like what the fuck do you think we are doing every day, just calling patients with bad insurance information? Idiot. We only verify insurance the day before, you know why? Because your insurance policy could change. This is especially true with Medicaid patients. Here is an example for you morons; It is December 31, 2019, you have Aetna, but on January 1, 2020, you get new insurance through your employer…. duh.

Bringing Friends to your appointment

This is only acceptable if they are not high or intoxicated and can act like an adult when they are waiting for you in the waiting room. Do not bring your high or intoxicated friends to your office appointment. If your intoxicated friend cannot behave in the waiting room, alone, he/she will be brought into the exam room with you. No exceptions.

Specimens

After something is cut out of you or taken off you or whatever, it is considered a "specimen." We do not just do a procedure and throw the "specimen" in the trash. Hello, dumbshit, we must send it off to an outside lab to find out what it is. The reason for this is because we do not have a pathologist in the office, nor do we have a lab. Do not call us when you get a bill from the lab and ask us what it is for.

You need to call the lab. If you are calling on *their* statement, then you need to call the number on *their* bill. NOT US. Do not call us and be a belligerent asshole to me when you tell me that, "the lab doesn't participate with your insurance" and you did not authorize us to send the specimen to any lab. We must send the specimens out to someone, a pathologist that can prepare the specimen on a slide, look at it under a microscope and then tell your physician what is wrong with you. That is how it works.

Covid -19 or Corona Virus

Covid is not our fault.

Quit coming into the office with attitude about Covid/Corona Virus. We are just as irritated with Covid as you are, probably more so, because "you people" keep bitching at us, like we created it in our petri dish in the back room, you know the lab we don't have and the bay where we keep all our samples, we never put out then spread it all over the fucking world and are just sitting in the office waiting to give it to you. We did not and we do not have any petri dishes.

Televisits or Telemedicine

The new norm during the beginning of the pandemic and still you the patient are not happy. Mind you, the office is closed, due to this thing called a pandemic, we are running on a skeleton crew. Three employees instead of seventeen and you are calling us being fuckers. You want to come in for an appointment, we offer you a televisits, you decline, stating you must come into the office, we tell you the office is closed, you turn into an asshole. You were an asshole to start with. What was I thinking!

Masks

You must wear a mask in our office. In fact, now that this lovely virus as made a guest appearance on the entire planet, mind you. You must wear them everywhere. If you choose not to wear a mask, that is perfectly fine, you just cannot come into our office. Do not act like, we just made up these rules to piss you off. Rest assured we did not, we leave that stupid shit to the government. Anyone that has been on the planet from March of 2020 to present, should be aware of the Corona Virus, Covid-19, or "rona" for short. If you do not know any of this, you are either living under a rock, do not own a tv or radio or the drugs you are taking are off the shelf amazing! If that is the case, I will need to know where you get them! Kidding, not kidding!

Please do not come into the office without mask and ask us if we sell masks. We do not sell masks and we do not want you in our office without a mask. In fact, the signage on the door clearly states, "No Mask, No Entry." Not sure how we can make this any clearer.

As Covid starts to slow down or takes on a new form, i.e., The Delta or Omnicron variant, if you are vaccinated, then you still have to wear a mask in any medical office, including ours. The signage is still as big as your fucking head on the door and for some reason you still come into the office and ask if you need to wear a mask? WTF. For our patients that come into the office without a mask, one will be provided for you. A pink one. That's right, we only have pink ones. I do not give a flying fuckball that you are of the male persuasion. You will still wear a pink mask, that is, if you want to be seen. I do not care that you sit out in the waiting room and complain to every patient in our waiting room. Lesson learned here, is wear YOUR OWN MASK DUMB FUCK.

Patients that are not our patients and just wander into our office and ask for a mask, what are you thinking? We are not going to give you a mask. You need to go to the office where you have the appointment and get a God Damn mask from them. What are you thinking?

To the man that came in and told my front desk girl that she was a miserable person because she would not supply you with a mask. You sir, and I use the word "sir" lightly are the miserable fucking idiot that gives all the other idiots a bad name on this planet. Fucking dickwad.

Waiting in Your Car

The pandemic has changed everything. The waiting room is now in your car. Feel free to treat it like you would our waiting room. You know, where you drop trash all over it, gum, sucker wrappers, Kleenex, and whatever else you are carrying that you want to get rid of.

Waiting in your car is not our fault. Physician offices around the country are all struggling with keeping a limited number of patients in the waiting room, conforming to CDC Guidelines that change almost hourly. Do not come into the office and bitch about this. You will be told we are doing the best we can, because we are doing the best we can. If you do not like that response, then you can leave. Wow a whole chapter and I did not say Fuck, which is quite amazing for me.

Covid Forms/Questions

These are just as much as a pain in the ass for us as they are for you. Just be nice and either fill out the form or answer the questions we ask you over the phone. Do not come in and be a fucker to us and ask us why we are asking the same questions when you were just here four days ago. The answer will be because we must, and besides, dickhead, we have no idea where you have been for the last four days and who you have been with or what the fuck you have been doing. Fill out the fucking form or answer the questions you are asked.

Trust me on this, no one in our office really wants to know if you lost your sense of smell, have had diarrhea, muscle aches, fever, chills or cannot taste or smell your diarrhea. Jesus, just answer the fucking questions.

When we ask you if you have had Covid, do not answer, "I'm not sure." This is an idiotic response and will get you landed in my office where I will have to ask you more questions. Either you know you have had the virus, or you do not have it.

If you answer "Yes" to have you had a positive Covid test, do not ask us why we need to know that. Again, I am thinking that the virus as severely affected your brain.

Do not tell us that you have Covid, but you feel fine and then want to come in for your visit. The answer will be No, it will never be yes, and it will be noted in your medical records that you came to the office knowing you had it. Then when you try to make another appointment, we will so pleasantly ask you if you have been re-tested and received a negative result. That is the only way you will be able to enter the office. This also goes for, "I've been exposed to Covid through a friend or family member." In short stay home, do not infect the rest of the world. You are the problem!

Covid forms must be filled out every fucking time you come into the office. Even if you were just in yesterday. When I hand you a form, please do not tell me the answer is "NO" to all the questions. That is awesome for you, but you are still going to be handed the fucking form and you *are* going to fill out the motherfucking thing.

Temperatures

Now that we are in the middle of a pandemic, we must take your temperature. Do not be a fuckstick about it, when you are asked to remove your hat or lift your hair away from your head, so that we can take your temperature on your forehead, just do it. You are not thinking about how lucky you really are. You see, I could be taking your temperature and not with that little handheld gun that the medical assistants shoot you in the head with. I could have a rectal thermometer. And trust me, nothing would give me greater pleasure than shoving that thing so far up your ass, your eyeballs pop out of your head.

See now, you will be so nice when you go see your physician and they will love it when they see you taking off your hat or moving your hair and everyone will be so happy. It is another wonderful day ☐.

This is all a great scenario if you have a normal temperature, but if you have a temperature over 100.3, you are fucked. You will be brought into a room, where the medical assistant will come back and take your temperature again, and again, and again. If it goes down after five minutes then, yippee, you can have your office visit, if it does not recede, well you get a personal escort out of the office and you will have to call your primary care physician.

Please do not tell us that you run hot. A fever of 103 degrees is not running hot. That is running to the Grim Reaper.

Plexiglass Dividers/Blue Tape

Six Foot Rule

All the precautions the office has put in place is not only for your protection, but also for ours. The blue tape on the floor that says, "Stand Here" in bold black ink, means that is where you need to stand, do not lean on the desks and be an Asswipe to the girls checking you in and out.

Do not tell them that you are just going to tip over the plexiglass on them or breath around them. I will make sure that I come out and run every fucking pen through my ass cheeks that is out there for you to use. But on a more positive note, with the plexiglass, I have found that none of the female patients are resting their tits on the desk!

A little side note to the plexiglass; is that not only can we see through it, but we can also actually hear through it. It's one of those magical times again. If we can hear through it, I will bet you, our beloved patient can also see & hear through it. Please do not bend down to the slot where we slide through your copay and any other information, remove your mask, and start talking to us. WTF?

Also do not come to the separation of the plexiglass and speak to me plain face. Sorry buddy but this is not going to work for me. I will make you chase me around that whole fucking office to a free piece of plexiglass that we can speak through. Dip shit.

Magazines During Covid-19

Here' s the beauty of Covid, we no longer have magazines for you to read, in fact, we don't have one fucking thing for you to read. Bring your own shit and again, do not complain that we do not have anything to read. How funny, with or without Covid, the complaining never stops. Before you did not like our selection of magazines and now that we do not have anything for you to read and you are still fucking complaining.

Sanitizing

It is being done in the office and just because you do not see it, does not mean it does not happen. Think of it like oxygen, you cannot see it but somehow you are all still alive. We are trying our best to ensure your safety as well as our own. Please do not ask to speak to me and berate me about how the front desk girls are not cleaning the waiting room. I want you to sit there, and really look at what is going on.   The phones are ringing, the patients are calling from their cars, no one can get through, everyone is frustrated, and you are in my office bitching to me that nothing is getting cleaned. I will listen intently, but if you feel the office is unsafe or unclean and you are going to die from Covid in our office, then what in the flying fucksausages are you doing out of your fucking house?

OSHA & THE CDC

If you are the mother fucker that felt it necessary to turn either one of our offices into The CDC or OSHA. I would like to tell you that I have a few choice words for you and none of them are nice. If you do not feel safe out in the Covid-19, pandemic world then you should not be in our office let alone out of your fucking house.

Back to the sanitizing section, we are doing it because we want to be safe and we want you, our beloved motherfucking Asswipe fucking patients to be safe as well. We clean the waiting rooms approximately every fifteen to twenty minutes and the exam rooms are cleaned in between patients and everything in the room is wiped down including the doorknobs and the switches on the wall. We are using the same cleaner that the hospitals use, so when you are going to make a complaint, you better know what the fuck you are talking about.

As for the employee that complained to OSHA that we were not following the six foot rule in our lab alcove and wouldn't give their name, well, you are a true piece of work, total chickenshit asshole.

I only had to write a five page essay to OSHA describing everything we clean in the office as well as how we clean it, what we use to clean it and how many times an hour we clean it. I may have even showed them how I clean my own asshole.

My secret advice to you is this, if you are afraid of coming to work, please quit or just stay the fuck home.

"How Did You Enjoy Your Six Weeks off?"

Did you just stand in front of me and ask me this? My non-verbal response is FUCK YOU BITCH. But with a sweet little smile that you cannot see, because I have a mask on, I gently tell you, we were open during the midst of the pandemic. For emergencies, surgeries, and injections. The moral of this little chapter is, think, you stupid fuck before you speak. Not all businesses were closed during the first outbreak of Covid.

Ungrateful Mother Fuckers

Do you know what Covid did? It somehow made all of you more ungrateful than you were before, which is something I still am trying to understand. We are in the middle of a Pandemic, and all is you can do is bitch at us because we have limited hours, you wanted a real appointment, but we were only doing televisits, this is not good enough and you want to come in. Sure, you can come in, but you are not going to see anyone, you know why? Cuz all the doctors, physician assistant or nurse practitioners are not in the fucking office, because it is a God Damn Pandemic!

Stupid Questions

Do not ask us if we know how long the Pandemic is going to last. Why would you even think for a second that we would have the answer to this? This is a Magic 8 Ball question. That is the thing you should ask. I have a good feeling that you will get all your questions answered from that thing, probably end up having a great conversation with that thing too. #Scaredforyou.

Magic 8 Ball Questions

When is it going to stop snowing?

When is the Pandemic going to be over with?

Why don't the paper drapes have strings?

Does bottled water expire? (I think this will be the title of my next book)

Pens and Covid

Covid is a terrible thing, but I find that no one wants our pens anymore! We have two containers on both the front and back desks, one that says, "clean pens" and one that says, "dirty pens." We have a lot of pens for you to steal but no one is taking them! You do not even want the clean ones. Crazy. Some days, I just want to take the dirty pens and put them in the clean container, tee hee hee.

Samples, Suckers, Lollipops

&

Covid

Hahahaha! Guess what?! If you think we are going to have the sample basket that we had out for your enjoyment, before Covid, you are seriously mistaken! If we do not have magazines for you, what makes you think we are going to hand out samples! Cracks me up all day long!

Oh, and that goes for suckers and Lollipops! Do not have those either! Bahahaha.

Do you know since Covid hit, I have not had to pick up one chewed up nasty, sticky sucker or lollipop of the floor? Honestly, I am kinda enjoying this pandemic.

Suggestions

Ahhh, where to do I start with this?

Prior to the pandemic, not one of you really gave a shit about anything but yourselves. Now that we have a pandemic, patients are just telling me all kinds of stupid shit.

Let us start with taking temperatures, shall we? To the gentleman that told us that "we should start taking temperature outside the office to keep everyone safe inside, you know like how the hospital does it." I want you to really think about this, really think.

The hospital has a staff of let us say twenty-five hundred, if not more people, they can spare one or two of them to stand at the door and take your temperature and give you hand sanitizer. As for this office, we have seventeen people in here That is it. They all have jobs that are essential to how the practice runs. We are not doing this. If you are not happy with this. Tough shit.

Hand sanitizer, we need to order a different kind, you do not like it. Bring your own then. We put it out as a courtesy. I do not give a rat's ass that you do not like it. We order it in bulk and the last thing on my mind when I order it is if you are going to like it or not. Give me a fucking break.

Do not tell me it is unsanitary to put it out the hand sanitizer on the front or back desk and every patient in the office is using it. Yes, that is the point. Again, if you do not like it, bring your own, or risk walking out of the office with dirty corona virus hands. Laughing on the inside ☺

Unlock the front door; When the office reaches its capacity, we must lock the front door because per the CDC guidelines we can only have so many people in our waiting room and office at a time. This is the reason the door is locked. Please do not keep pulling and pushing on the door, knocking on the glass, like we do not see your sorry asses. We can see you but you trying to knock the door down is not going to get you in the office any quicker than waiting in your car. We will call you when it is your turn to be seen.

There are too many people in the waiting room; This one kills me. We have had to turn our chairs around so that people do not sit in them. Please do not turn them back around and sit in them. We will come out to the waiting room and ask you to move. Do not come into the waiting room and stand in front of the door with attitude. When I ask you to sit down, sit your fucking ass down in a chair or risk me smashing you between the door and the wall. Honesty, nothing would give me greater pleasure than doing this myself and watching you bleed out on our newly finished floors.

I cannot tell you how many times I have had the same conversation with patients about the capacity in the office. I even had one patient tell me that they were going to write a letter to their doctor. Oh, please let me get you a pen that I have just swiped through my ass and a piece of paper now.

Picking up Lab Orders, Forms or Results

If you are doing any of the things above and you have specifically called us to pick up a lab orders, finished forms or test results. Then we expect you to come and get the God Damn things. If they are left and not picked up within a certain time frame, they are shredded. We are not in the business of calling to remind you to come get them, nor will we do that. Come and get them or they are gone. You should also be aware that it will be noted in your chart that you did not come and get it, so when you call again after six months telling us, "That you totally forgot to come get them, and are they still there?" We can tell you with a smile under our masks that, "that no, we've already shredded them. Do not ask us to mail anything. The answer will be NO and will never be yes.

Are you calling for your child?

It is one thing if you are calling for your ten-year-old or your seventeen-year-old, but if you are calling for your thirty-three-year-old for anything, we will not talk to you.

First, What the fuck, wtf, wtf? Do not call the office and tell me you are calling for your forty-five-year-old son because he is too busy to call, and he needs his prescription. No, no and no. He needs to call unless he is handicapped or has, condition where he cannot call us.

Being in another state on business does count for being handicapped or having a medical condition by the way. The only way we will ever speak to you is if the form where your child has authorized us to speak to you. Do not act all high and mighty and get insulted when we go to access that on our system. It is called HIPPA. -Health Insurance Portability and Accountability

Act. What this means, is that if your kid did not say we can talk to you. We will not.

I think this form is one of my favorites! Laughing on the inside again. Do not try to tell me your listed on it when I am looking at it and you are not. This little form is filled out by everyone, including your eighteen-year-old children, because they are no longer considered children. They are adults. See the minor's chapter!

The Trash

Do I really have to have this chapter in my book? Do not bring your children's dirty diapers to our office and think you are going to just a throw a shitty diaper in our trash. Who does this? And why do you think it is ok? It is not. Keep your kid's shit wrapped in a plastic bag and throw it away outside or better yet when you get home. Nothing is worse than smelling baby diarrhea all day and wondering where it is coming from. I think you are the people that are destroying our bathrooms. WTF Really? You are probably thinking this is heartless and I am just the biggest bitch on the planet. I get that all babies shit and all, but come on, be a responsible person and dispense of it somewhere else.

Covid and your appointment

As the pandemic starts to slow down, we can see you back in the office now. If you are here for an appointment and lucky enough to have a room made available for you. Do not be an asshole to us. Do not tell us that you have just waited thirty minutes in your car, and you do not have air conditioning and it is one hundred degrees in your car. This is your new waiting room and the reality of life. Tough shit.

When you get past the taking of your temperature and you are brought to an exam room, the same rules apply as is if we were not in the middle of a pandemic.

If you have a rash on your face, then you will have to remove your mask. Do not act like an asshole to me when I ask you to remove your mask so that medical assistant Lori can see your fucking face. Please do not assume that I have ESP or x-ray vision. I do not. I just want to see your fucking face.

MIPS

I know, none of you know what this is, but MIPS stands for Merit-Based Incentive Payment System. Now what this means to you, our lovely patients, is Medical Assistant Lori is going to ask you some questions and you are going to try your absolute best not to be a fuck sausage and answer them.

Some offices ask you if you feel safe at home, can you afford your prescriptions, blah blah blah. You answer them without giving any thought. But when I ask you if you drink alcohol or smoke, do not answer with another question, or tell me your whole fucking life story. I just want to know if you drink or smoke. I am not looking for what kind of cigarettes you smoke or what kind of weed, I just want to know if you smoke.

When I ask you if you drink alcohol and you must reason why and what kind of alcohol you are drinking; that has nothing to do with me. I just want to know if you drink. Wine, just so you know IS considered alcohol by the way.

Please, when you tell me you drink wine, but it is not really an alcoholic drink, this is a problem. More for you than for me.

When I ask you if you have had your flu shot or pneumovax injection, please do not ask me, "for this year?" No asshole for ten years ago! Of course, it is for this year, idiot.

If you are over the age of sixty-five, there are different questions, such as, "Have you discussed an advanced care proxy with someone in your home?" Again, not looking for your whole life story, just a yes or no.

For adolescent children, we have questions for you too. Parents: do not answer for your kid if you are in the exam room with them. I am not asking you these questions; I am asking these questions of your child. Same as the big patient questions, "Do you drink, smoke, flu shot, etc." Do not answer for them. I am not interested in your answer and if you answer for them, the questions will be redirected to them point blankly while you are in the room with them.

For patients that are total assholes and will not answer any of these questions and think the government has some secret plan for all your idiot answers. I can assure you, they, like the rest of us do not give a royal fuck.

MIPS is how all your physicians are getting paid. From all your idiotic fucking answers. The Centers for Medicare are the ones that produced this brilliant concept of how we can piss off our patients more by asking them questions no one cares about, including us. At the end of the year, all our points are tallied up from all these questions and other measures and that is how we are paid. Do not be fuckers because you think we are just asking these questions for no reason.

Cell Phones

This is a huge issue for me, as I can barely keep my staff off their cell phones and now, you are going to walk into the office talking on your cell phone? No, no & NO. Put that mother fucker away and act accordingly. It is so rude to check in while you are speaking to whomever and my front desk girls are trying to check you in. They are speaking to you, trying to compile accurate information and all you can do is ignore them and take the paperwork and walk away. You, Mr., Ms., Mrs. shithead, will wait and wait if I have my say.

Procedures and Surgeries

Let us talk about surgeries, which by the way are a hot commodity. We only have one surgeon, that only does surgery once a week. He is triple booked most days. Prior to your upcoming surgery you are called and reminded about your surgery, one to two days prior to the surgery.

We MUST speak to you. You are the only one that can confirm the surgery. If you are handicapped or one hundred years old, then of course your family member can do it. Do not confirm an appointment you have no intention of coming to. It will piss off the office staff as well as your surgeon and if you think for one second, we are just going to reschedule you for the next appointment, you are sadly mistaken.

Yearly Exams

A yearly exam is just that, "YEARLY." Please do not tell me you are here for your three-month yearly exam. I hope you realize just how fucking stupid you sound.

Yearly exams, physicals, whatever, are done on a yearly basis. We are talking every three hundred and sixty-five days you, our beloved patient can come in and have a physical or yearly exam of some type.

Your insurance will only allow one physical or yearly exam a year. Again, that means you only get to come in once in a year for a yearly exam.

Do not try to tell me that your insurance will pay for two yearly exams, trust me they will not. Besides the fact if you had two yearly exams, in one year, how ridiculous does that sound. Moron.

Sometimes if you have a certain condition, your insurance will allow you to be seen twice in one year for your condition, but it will not be coded as an annual or yearly exam. One visit will be coded as a yearly exam the other will be coded as a follow up or whatever your condition is.

Yearly exams are not free. I'm not sure where this reasoning comes from and I don't care either. If you have a copay, you will pay a copay do not try to tell us this is your free visit.

Medical Coding

Please do not call my biller to tell her that she coded your services wrong. Chances are she did not. Also do not call and tell us that your insurance says we coded it wrong. We did not. The reason they are telling you this is because they want us to change the code to a payable code. We will not do this. And we will tell you this. We go by your medical records and if it did not happen in the medical record, then it is not going to happen with us changing it to make it so that your insurance will pay it.

Also do not call us to tell us you are a new patient, and you are having a non-billable office visit or procedure and your insurance will pay it!

I need you to listen to yourself for a minute when you say this stupid shit. If it is a non-billable visit of any kind, no one is going to pay for it, except you. We will not bill it out to your insurance, and we will not send out a bill to you. YOU will pay it at the time of service. No statement will be sent. You know why because it is a non-billable service which means there are no CPT codes for your situation. (Current Procedural Terminology) If there are no CPT codes then no one on the planet can bill it out.

Do not ask us to bill it out to your insurance, we will not. This also applies to, "My insurance company says they will pay it if you use this code blah blah blah." Ok we can use the code you give us, but you will pay in full for your procedure or service, we will bill it out to your insurance and wait for them to deny it.

This is how it works, every time. Do not call me and tell me we cannot do this. We can and we do. Also do not threaten me by saying, "I'm going to call my insurance company." Because here is what I am going to say is, "Come on in my office, we can call them together!" Mother Fucker.

"It's Covered"

When you hear this from your provider, whether it be the doctor, the nurse practitioner, or the physician Assistant or whomever for that matter, it means your insurance will cover it. But let me be noticeably clear, if you get a bill from us after you have been told, "Your services are covered," and you have a deductible, do not for one second think we are going to write it off. In our eyes it was and is covered. Just because they put it towards your deductible has NOTHING to do with it not being covered.

You should know your benefits before you ever set one foot in any doctor's office. It is not the responsibility of any staff member in any physician's office to know YOUR insurance benefits. Dumbshit.

"Do you take my insurance?"

Oh, Sweet Baby Jesus, please do not call us and ask us this. For starters we take well over five hundred insurances, probably more. We take one kind of insurance with three hundred versions of it under the umbrella. Calling us and asking us if we take your insurance, is an extremely bad idea. Call your insurance company and ask them if they participate with your provider, which is the best thing to do.

However, some insurances do not have access to their entire profile of all the policies we do and do not take, and will just tell you yes, we take it when in fact we do not.

Do not call me and be a fuckstick telling me we take your insurance when in fact we do not.

You see I do all the credentialing for my providers, and I know which insurances we take and the three-hundred versions of the five-hundred companies, I know which ones we take and which ones we do not.

Do not get all bent out of shape when I tell you we do not participate with your insurance and if you want to come in, you will either need to pay out of pocket or find out if you have out of network benefits. I am doing you a favor and giving you all the information up front like a nice person, asshole. Also do not tell me you have never heard of a doctor's office not participating in your plan. What?

As any physician's office will tell you, we must negotiate our contracts with your shitty insurance companies for payment of services. This is how it works. We just do not participate with all the insurance companies on the planet.

We like getting paid for services rendered and if we cannot come to an agreement with an insurance company on payment of services, then we are not going to participate with the insurance and therefore, we will be non-par or out of network.

The Friend Card

Please don't call the office and tell us you are the doctor's friend. We don't care. And you want an appointment for a specific day and time. It won't work. You'd be amazed at how many times patients tell us, "I'm the doctor's friend," and we go speak to your doctor or other health care provider and then after we tell them that you are their friend, they look at us like we have three heads. Only patients that are not really their friends play this card. Don't try to tell me when you call that you are his/her friend and you shouldn't have a copay or have to pay your deductible, because every time we ask, we are told we do not adjust off copays or deductibles, regardless of if you are a friends or not.

The Race Card

First and foremost, we do not discriminate against anyone. All patients are treated with dignity, respect and kindness. Even for me, I would never want anyone to feel disrespected for anything, let alone the color of their skin.

Please do not call in when you do not like our rules or policies to tell me that the front desk girl is a racist. This will not set well with me. Not one staff member or the physician staff are racist.

Do not tell me that you knew we were a racist practice when you only saw white women and white men sitting in our office and you immediately knew what kind of office we were. Who says that shit? Some one that is a belligerent mother fucker that's who. Now for your next visit, I'll make sure to hire black and latino actors to sit in our waiting room and look sick. Dumb fuck.

Students

We are a teaching practice, which means your provider has signed up to teach medical students. If this is your provider, he or she will NEVER run on time, EVER.

What you can do as a patient, is two things; you can be patient and just suck it up or you can change providers. Don't be a fucker to us, we have no control over this and honestly, your provider is training a future physician in the field, how do you think doctors become doctors, idiot.

Students, when you come to work at our practice, let's try and remember a few things. You're not actually an employee of our practice, you are a guest. When the provider you are shadowing tells you to call a patient and leave them a message, don't call them and say, "Hi this is Sally from blah blah practice calling with your test results."

What happens is the patient calls back and asks for Sally and everyone that answers the phone is like who the Fuck is Sally? What you need to say when you are calling and leaving a message is, "This is Sally, I am the student and I have your test results from your biopsy you had with Dr blah blah."

Another thing to remember is, you are not the doctor, you are the student. Don't tell my employees what to fucking do. That's my job and if I hear you are telling my employees what to do, you will no longer be a student in our practice.

Here's my favorite one; if you are the fucking bitchface patient that recently wreaked havoc on the practice and complained and complained about not getting your prescription in a timely manner, you know the one that needed a prior authorization, then had your mommy call us too, then turned around and wrote a nasty comment on Yelp and has turned into a student, well you may be wondering why we all hate you and treat you like shit. It was a short stint for you, and we all hope that you picked up on how much we hated you. Yeah, that karma thing, it's a bitch baby, ain't it.

Oh, and by the way, the seventeen employees in our practice including the one that you shadowed, will never come to see you as a physician, should you literally pass the exam that is.

Drug Reps

Drug reps are a necessity of any practice. We as a medical group count on them to deliver samples of prescription medication.

They bring us samples of medications, they bring us breakfast, lunch, snacks and more, and we literally love you guys. Most of you that is.

Don't overstay your welcome. It doesn't take two hours to drop off samples get a physician signature. I know you think my medical assistants have nothing to do but talk to you, but that is a fallacy. As for talking to my providers for two hours in between patients, well, there is a point where I'm going to come back to where you are and say, "get the fuck out". Most of you that know me, know this is true. I don't mix my words and I'll never sugar coat anything.

GREAT PATIENTS

I've saved the best for last. I cannot tell you how much you are appreciated.
Patients that are wonderful, make our day. From just treating the staff like
humans, to bringing in goodies for the staff and providers. We cannot thank
you enough. Even speaking to a nice patient on the phone is amazing and we
talk and talk about how lovely you are and how much we love you.

When one of you lovely people walk in with doughnuts or even a bag of
candy, or the man that brings in peppers from his garden, this completely
melts our hearts. There are so many of you out there, the man that cans his
own strawberry jam and brings it in, wonderful stuff! To the lady that brings
in the delicious bakery confections, thank you! To the man that brings in
chocolate Easter bunnies, we love you! To the lady that brought me a Dunkin'
Doughnuts Gift card, thank you! Or the lady I helped get a PA for and gave
me a beautifully handmade stuffed reindeer, I love it. To the lady that brings

us Christmas cookies, we love you, we eat them 'til they're gone! Which doesn't take long, by the way.

You are the patients that I can only hope the other shit heads can aspire too.

I hope you know that when you bring in something for us or simply treat us with dignity, you have truly made our day golden. YOU ARE SO APPRECIATED.

Some Final Thoughts
And Such

You know this book could go on and on because every day some asshole walks in and does something stupid. I used to say nothing surprises me anymore, but that seems to be a total lie!

All good things must come to an end, right?

I would like to add just a few things, though. I thank God every day for my wonderful staff, even though we may not get everything right every day we do try our best to take care of you, our beloved patients. Every person in our office shows up to take care of you, the nice patients and the asshole patients, remember that.

Your doctor's office and the employees that show up when they are sick, their families are sick, have cancer, are dying, there's a pandemic, still come to work to care for YOU.

Don't be a fucking asshole to us.

I'm hoping by now you have figured out with a little help from these past chapters of what not what to do when you have your next visit with your doctor, nurse practitioner or physician assistant.

As a final note, I'd like to remind all of you, that since you have filled out all our paperwork with your correct information, we know where you live.

Let that sink in.

I'm a crazy bitch when I want to be, bahahahaha.